Published By Robert Corbin

@ Travis Frye

Low-FODMAP Cookbook: Healthy Low-FODMAP

Diet Plan & Manage Your IBS Symptoms And

Improve Your Gut

ISBN 978-87-94477-07-9

AF367126

TABLE OF CONTENTS

What are FDMAPs?

Have yu ever felt like yur digestive system has a mind f its wn, playing tricks n yu just when yu least expect it?

Well, my dear wmen , yu're nt alne. Many wmen ut there have experienced the frustrating and ften uncmfrtable symptms f digestive issues. But fear nt, fr I have just the slutin fr yu — the Lw FDMAP Diet!

Nw, befre we dive headfirst int the tantalizing recipes and muthwatering dishes that await yu in this ckbk, let's take a mment t unravel the mystery behind FDMAPs. I knw, I knw, it sunds like sme strange acrnym frm a secret sciety, but I prmise yu, it's nt that cmplicated.

FDMAPs, my dear reader, stands fr Fermentable ligsaccharides, Disaccharides, Mnsaccharides, and Plyls.

Whew, that's a muthful! But dn't wrry, yu wn't need t memrize this tngue-twister. In essence, FDMAPs are a grup f carbhydrates and sugar alchls fund in certain fds that can wreak havc n ur delicate digestive systems.

Imagine yur gut as a bustling city, with tiny wrkers diligently breaking dwn the fd yu eat. Well, FDMAPs are like mischievus trublemakers in this bustling city. They can ferment in yur gut, causing blating, gas, abdminal pain, and ther nt-s-fun symptms. N wnder yu've been feeling like yur tummy has turned int a ht air balln!

But here's the gd news — the Lw FDMAP Diet can cme t yur rescue! It's nt a fad r a passing trend; it's a scientifically-backed apprach designed t help yu identify and eliminate the specific trigger fds that may be causing yur digestive distress. By fllwing this dietary plan, yu can gain cntrl ver yur symptms and start living life t the fullest nce again.

S, my lvely reader, prepare yurself fr an exciting culinary adventure thrugh the wrld f lw FDMAP cking. In the chapters that fllw, we'll explre a treasure trve f delectable recipes tailred especially fr wmen like yu. Frm muthwatering breakfast delights t cmfrting dinner feasts and everything in between, this ckbk will be yur trusted cmpanin n yur jurney t better digestive health.

Remember, yu're nt alne in this. I'll be right here with yu, guiding yu every step f the way. Tgether, we'll embark n a flavrful and nurishing vyage, embracing the Lw FDMAP Diet with pen arms. S, let's gather ur ingredients, dn ur aprns, and get ready t create delicius dishes that will make yur taste buds dance with jy!

Lw FDMAP Smthie Bwl

Ingredients:

- 1 tablespn chia seeds

- 1/4 cup gluten-free granla

- 1/4 cup mixed berries (strawberries, blueberries, raspberries)

- 1/2 cup refrigerated mixed berries (strawberries, blueberries, raspberries)

- 1/2 ripe banana

- 1/2 cup lactse-free ygurt

- 1 tablespn almnd butter

Directins:

1. In a blender, blend tgether the frzen mixed berries, banana, lactse-free ygurt, and almnd butter until smth.

2. Pur the smthie int a bwl.

3. Tp with chia seeds, gluten-free granla, and mixed berries.

Lw FDMAP Breakfast Tacs

Ingredients:

- 1/4 cup diced green nin (green part nly)
- 1 tablespn live il
- Salt and pepper
- Salsa and cilantr fr serving
- 2 gluten-free trtillas
- 2 eggs, scrambled
- 1/4 cup diced red bell pepper

Directins:

1. Heat the cking il in a nn-stick pan ver medium heat temperature.

2. Add the red bell pepper and green nin and ck fr 2-3 minutes until sftened.

3. Add the scrambled eggs and ck fr anther 2-3 minutes until set.

4. Warm the gluten-free trtillas in the micrwave r n a pan.

5. Spn the egg mixture nt the trtillas and tp with salsa and cilantr.

Carrt Cake with Pecans

Ingredients:

- 200g gluten-free self-rising flur

- 1 tsp cinnamn

- 1 tsp gluten-free baking pwder

- 50g pecans, chpped

- 140g unsalted butter, sftened, plus extra fr greasing

- 200g caster sugar

- 250g carrts, grated

- 140g sultanas

- 2 eggs, lightly beaten

Fr the icing

- 175g icing sugar

- 3 tsp cinnamn plus extra fr dusting

- 75g butter, sftened

Directins:

1. Heat ven t 350F. Grease and line a 2 lb bread laf pan with baking parchment.
2. Beat the butter and sugar with a mixer until sft and fluffy, then add the grated carrt and sultanas. Add the eggs int the mixing bwl ne at a time, scraping and stirring after each additin.
3. Add the flur, cinnamn, baking pwder and mst f the chpped pecans and mix well. Pur the mix int the laf tin, then bake fr 50-55 mins r until a knife inserted in the middle cmes ut clean. Allw t cl in the pan fr 15 mins, then remve frm the pan and cl cmpletely n a wire rack.
4. While the laf cake is baking, make the icing. Let the butter cme t rm temperature, until it is sft. Whip the butter in a large bwl until it has dubled in vlume, add the icing sugar and cinnamn, and then beat until the icing is thick

and creamy. When the cake is cl t the tuch,
spread the icing n tp, then sprinkle with
cinnamn in a decrative pattern and drizzle the
remaining chpped nuts.

Frittata with Spinach and Ham

Ingredients:

- 1/2 cup pure cream r lactse free milk

- 1/3 cup grated parmesan cheese

- 250g cherry tmates, halved

- 1 bunch spinach, trimmed, shredded

- 100g ham, chpped

- 6 eggs

Directins:

1. Preheat the ven t 375F. Place parchment paper int an 8 x 8 glass pan. Grease the parchment paper and make sure there is a 2 inch verhang n 2 f the sides.

2. Layer half f the spinach int the pan. Tp with half f the ham. Cntinue t layer the spinach and the ham. There shuld be fur layers ttal.

3. Mix the eggs, cheese, and milk r milk
    substitute int a bwl, cmbining thrughly. Add
    salt and pepper and pur ver the tp f the
    spinach and ham. Arrange the tmates n tp,
    with the cut sides upturned.

4. Bake 35 t 40 minutes until glden brwn and the
    eggs are set. Rest 10 minutes befre cutting.
    Serve with gluten free rlls r tast and a small
    serving f strawberries r raspberries n the side.

Carrt Cake with Pecans

Ingredients:

- 2 eggs, lightly beaten

- 200g gluten-free self-rising flur

- 1 tsp cinnamn

- 1 tsp gluten-free baking pwder

- 50g pecans, chpped

- 140g unsalted butter, sftened, plus extra fr greasing

- 200g caster sugar

- 250g carrts, grated

- 140g sultanas

Fr the icing

- 75g butter, sftened

- 175g icing sugar

- 3 tsp cinnamn plus extra fr dusting

Directins:

1. Heat ven t 350F. Grease and line a 2 lb bread laf pan with baking parchment.

2. Beat the butter and sugar with a mixer until sft and fluffy, then add the grated carrt and sultanas. Add the eggs int the mixing bwl ne at a time, scraping and stirring after each additin.

3. Add the flur, cinnamn, baking pwder and mst f the chpped pecans and mix well. Pur the mix int the laf tin, then bake fr 50-55 mins r until a knife inserted in the middle cmes ut clean. Allw t cl in the pan fr 15 mins, then remve frm the pan and cl cmpletely n a wire rack.

4. While the laf cake is baking, make the icing. Let the butter cme t rm temperature, until it is sft. Whip the butter in a large bwl until it has

dubled in vlume, add the icing sugar and cinnamn, and then beat until the icing is thick and creamy. When the cake is cl t the tuch, spread the icing n tp, then sprinkle with cinnamn in a decrative pattern and drizzle the remaining chpped nuts.

Dark Chclate Granla

Ingredients:

- 7 tablespns live il

- ½ cup dried ccnut, shredded

- 2 teaspns vanilla extract

- 7 tablespns Dutch cca pwder

- 5 tablespns pure maple syrup

- 5 tablespns brwn sugar

- 3 cups quina flakes

- 1/8 teaspn sea salt

- 2 cups quina puffs

- 100 grams dark chclate, chpped

- 3 cups pumpkin and sunflwer seeds, chpped

Directins:

1. Set up the ven t 120 degrees Celsius.

2. Place quina flakes, brwn sugar, quina puffs, pumpkin and sunflwer seeds, cca pwder and dried ccnut in a large bwl. Mix well.

3. In a separate bwl, pur vanilla extract, live il and maple syrup. Stir well.

4. Cmbine the tw mixtures thrughly.

5. Line tw rasting trays using baking paper. Spread the granla mixture n the trays evenly.

6. Place the trays in the ven and bake fr abut 20 minutes. Stir r give it a shake befre placing it back int the ven and letting it ck fr anther 15 minutes.

7. Afterwards, sprinkle sea salt and dark chclate n tp and put it in the ven fr anther 5 minutes.

8. nce dne, take the granla ut f the ven and allw it t cl fr abut an hur r tw. Stre it in airtight cntainers r jars.

Banana French Tast

Ingredients:

- 40 grams cmmn, firm banana, sliced

- 2 teaspns cinnamn, grund

- 3 teaspns pure maple syrup

- ½ dairy-free butter r live il spread

- 2 slices spelt surdugh r wheat bread

- 2 pecans, crumbled

- 1 egg

Directins:

1. Whisk the egg tgether with cinnamn in a wide bwl with a flat bttm.

2. Sak the bread slices with the egg mixture ne at a time. Make sure that bth slices are cmpletely cvered with the mixture.

3. Put butter in a large fry pan and place it ver medium heat. Ck the saked bread in the pan fr abut 2 minutes.

4. Flip the bread and ck until tasty and slightly brwn in clr.

5. Serve with pecans, banana and a drizzle f maple syrup.

Breakfast Wrap

NGREDIENTS:

- 2 cups spinach leaves

- ½ cup avocado

- 4 corn tortillas

- 8 slices cheddar cheese

DIRECTIONS:

1. Remove the shell from avocado and mash in a glass dish.
2. Rinse spinach leaves and shake to remove excess water.
3. Arrange tortillas on a flat surface.
4. Evenly divide and layer avocado, spinach leaves, and cheddar cheese on each.
5. Rotate to enclose, starting at the base.
6. Enjoy immediately.

Cinnamon Almond Crepes

INGREDIENTS:

- 1 cup almond milk, separated

- ¼ Tsp. ground cinnamon

- 2.67 tbsp. extra virgin olive oil, separated

- ½ cup almond flour*

- 2 medium bananas

- ¼ Tsp. pure vanilla extract, sugar-free

DIRECTIONS:

1. Empty 2 teaspoons of olive oil into a skillet and allow it to warm up.

2. In the meantime, blend almond milk, bananas, vanilla extract, cinnamon, and almond flour in a glass dish with an electric beater for 45 seconds.

3. Transfer a ladle of batter to the pan and swirl it around to distribute it evenly around.

4. Heat for 30 seconds or until edges turn
   darker, then turn to the other side.

5. Warm for an additional 30 seconds, then
   transfer to a serving platter. Enclose with tin
   foil.

6. Empty another 2 teaspoons in the skillet and
   repeat steps 3 through 6 until you have
   completed 8 crepes.

7. Enjoy immediately with your favorite fruits or
   compote.

Almond Butter & Banana Muffins

Ingredients

- ½ cup / 55g coconut flour

- 2 tsp cinnamn

- ½ tsp nutmeg

- 1 tsp baking powder

- 1 tsp bicarbonate of soda

- Pinch f sea salt

- 4 bananas

- 4 eggs

- ½ cup / 125g almond butter

- 2 tbsp coconut il, melted

- 1 tsp vanilla

Directins:

1. Preheat the ven t 180C, gas mark 4. Line a
   muffin tin with cases. In a blender or food

processor combine bananas, eggs, almond butter, coconut il, and vanilla.

2. Add in the coconut flur, cinnamn, nutmeg, baking pwder, soda, and salt. Blend into the wet mixture, scraping dwn the sides with a spatula.

3. Spn int the muffin cases.

4. Bake for 20-25 minutes, until a toothpick comes ut clean.

5. Best stred in the fridge or frzen

1. VARIATINS – cocoa powder is FDMAP friendly – use 1tbsp. You culd als stir in 2tbsp chopped walnuts to the mixture if wished.

Quina Protein Porridge

Ingredients

- 1 banana, sliced

- ½ teaspn grund cinnamon

- 1 teaspoon vanilla extract

- 1 tablespoon ground flaxseed

- 1 cup dairy free milk – almnd or ccnut (check labels)

- 1 cup water

- ½ cup quinoa

Directins:

1. Rinse the quinoa under cold running water.

2. Place the quinoa and water in a pan and bring to the boil.

3. Reduce the heat then cver and ck fr 10 minutes until just soft.

4. Add the milk, banana, cinnamn, flaxseeds, protein if using and vanilla.

5. Cook for 5 minutes until creamy. Add a little

mre milk if needed for a creamier texture.

6. Spoon into serving bowls.

Butternut Squash / Pumpkin and Cinnamn Granla

Ingredients

- ½ cup / 60g coconut oil melted

- 2 Tbsp maple syrup

- 1tbsp vanilla extract

- Pinch of sea salt

- 115g / ½ cup pumpkin or butternut squash pureed from a can or you can bake in the oven then puree

- 2 tsp ground cinnamon

- Serve with mixed berries and ccnut yogurt or soy 1 cup / 125g quina flakes, buckwheat flakes r gluten free oats (*for pale ptin use 1 cup grund almonds)

- 180g / 1½ cup sliced / flaked almonds

- 70g / 1 cup unsweetened coconut flakes

- 125g / 1 cup pumpkin seeds r mixture of seeds e.g sunflwer, sesame and pumpkin

- 2tbsp flaxseed grund

- 125g / 1 cup walnuts, chpped

- ygurt

Directins:

1. Preheat the oven to 180C, gas mark 4 and line a baking sheet with parchment paper.

2. In a large bowl combine flakes (or grund almnd), coconut flakes, almonds, pumpkin seeds and pecans.

3. In a blender, combine the pumpkin, coconut oil, maple syrup and cinnamon.

4. Add the wct ingredients to the dry ingredients and stir until dry ingredients are thrughly cated.

5. Spread the granola in a thin layer n the baking sheet.

6. Cook for 30 minutes stirring occasionally to prevent burning.

Green Tea Smoothie

INGREDIENTS

- 2 Ripe Bananas

- 1 teaspoon matcha (green tea pwder), or

- more to taste

- 4 teaspoons of maple syrup

- 8 tablespoons f lactse-free

- yogurt50 cl f lactose-free r

- almond milk

DIRECTINS:

1. Crush the banana on a saucer,

2. Add the matcha and put it in the glass f the

1. blender orkitchen mixer.

2. Add the maple syrup, yogurt and milk.

3. Blend for 1 or 2 minutes at high speed t

4. btain a homogeneous mixture.

5. To serve

Tomato And Feta Cheese Salad

I

NGREDIENTS

- radishes

- Salt

- Pepper

- 2 tablespoons of vinaigrette sauce

- 2 cucumbers

- 10g dill, or other armatic herbs (mint,

- coriander,etc.)

- 12

DIRECTINS:

1. Cut the cucumbers into sticks, drain well,

2. Sprinkle them with salt and let them

1. drain fr about 15 minutes.

2. Rinse and dry well.

3. Meanwhile, chop the dill and put it in a bowl.

4. Slice the radishes and add them.

5. Add the cucumbers too.

6. Seasn with a pinch f salt, a little pepper and

7. the vinaigrette sauce.

8. Mix and serve

Watercress And Orange Salad

INGREDIENTS

- 1 teaspn of mustard

- Salt Pepper

- 1 bunch of watercress

- 12 teaspoon f pink pepper (ptinal)

- 1 orange

- 2 spoons f extra virgin olive oil

- 1 tablespoon f vinegar

DIRECTINS:

1. Wash and dry the oranges and then grate the

1. peel.

2. Put the grated peel in a bowl.

3. Add the oil, vInegar and mustard.

4. Beat everything with a frk.

5. Add a pinch of salt and pepper.

6. Wash and dry the cress and place it on plates.

7. Peel the oranges, divide the wedges and

8.   arrange them on plates.

9.   Pour the sauce ver it, and garnish with pink

Banana atcakes

Ingredients:

- 1 tablespn hney (ptinal, fr added sweetness)

- 1 teaspn cinnamn

- 1/2 teaspn vanilla extract

- Pinch f salt

- Ccnut il (fr cking)

- 2 ripe bananas

- 1 cup rlled ats

- 2 tablespns almnd butter (r any nut butter f yur chice)

Directins:

1. In a medium-sized mixing bwl, mash the ripe bananas with a frk until smth.

2. Add the rlled ats, almnd butter, hney (if using), cinnamn, vanilla extract, and a pinch f salt t the bwl.

3. Mix well until all the ingredients are thrughly cmbined and frm a sticky batter.

4. Heat a nn-stick skillet r frying pan ver medium
    heat and add a small amunt f ccnut il t
    prevent sticking.

5. Spn a small amunt f the batter nt the heated
    skillet, frming small rund pancakes. Yu can
    adjust the size accrding t yur preference.

6. Ck the atcakes fr abut 2-3 minutes n each
    side, r until they turn glden brwn. Flip them
    carefully using a spatula t ensure even cking.

7. nce bth sides are cked t yur desired level f
    crispness, transfer the atcakes t a plate and
    cntinue

Gluten-free banana pancakes with almnd butter and maple syrup:

Ingredients:

- 1/4 teaspn baking pwder

- 1/4 teaspn cinnamn

- 1 tablespn almnd butter

- 1 tablespn maple syrup

- 1 ripe banana, mashed

- 2 eggs

- 1/4 cup almnd flur

Directins:

1. In a bwl, whisk tgether the mashed banana and eggs.

2. Add the almnd flur, baking pwder, and cinnamn, and mlx until well cmbined.

3. Heat a nn-stick skillet ver medium heat.

4. Spn the batter nt the skillet, making 2-3 pancakes.

5. Ck until bubbles frm n the surface f the
    pancakes, then flip and ck until glden brwn n
    bth sides.

6. Serve the pancakes tpped with almnd butter
    and maple syrup.

Sweet ptat and egg hash with gluten-free tast:

Ingredients:

- Salt and pepper t taste

- 2 slices gluten-free bread

- 1 sweet ptat, diced

- 2 eggs

- 1 tablespn butter r il

Directins:

1. Heat the butter r il in a nn-stick skillet ver medium heat.

2. Add the diced sweet ptat and sauté until tender and lightly brwned.

3. Crack the eggs int the skillet and ck, stirring ccasinally, until scrambled and cked thrugh.

4. Seasn with salt and pepper t taste.

5. Tast the gluten-free bread slices and serve alngside the sweet ptat and egg hash.

Gluten-free breakfast pizza with scrambled eggs, turkey bacn, and cheese:

Ingredients:

- 2 slices turkey bacn, chpped
- 1/2 cup shredded cheese
- Salt and pepper t taste
- 1 gluten-free pizza crust
- 2 eggs

Directins:

1. Preheat the ven t 425°F.
2. Ck the turkey bacn in a skillet ver medium heat until crispy.
3. In a separate skillet, scramble the eggs ver medium heat until cked thrugh.
4. Seasn the eggs with salt and pepper t taste.
5. Spread the shredded cheese n the gluten-free pizza crust.
6. Tp with the scrambled eggs and chpped turkey bacn.

7. Bake in the preheated ven fr 8-10 minutes,
    until the cheese is melted and bubbly.

8. Slice and serve ht.

Vegan Tuna Salad in Cllard Green Wraps

Ingredients

- 1 1/2 cups raw walnuts

- 1 cup pitted Kalamata lives

- ¼ cup seaweed or sea veggies (I used dried wakame)

- 2 celery stalks coarsely chopped

- 2 tablespns Bubbie's relish (I used sauerkraut, since it's what I had)

- 16 collard green leaves stems remved

- 2 heirloom tomatoes thinly sliced

- 1 tablespoon fresh chopped chives ptinal

Directins:

1. In a fd prcessr, pulse the walnuts until mealy. Add the olives, sea veggies, and relish (or kraut). Process again until a coarse paste. (Yu

might have to add a tablespoon or two of water to get it smooth).

2. Transfer the mixture to a medium mixing bowl and fld in the chopped celery.

3. Stack tw collard green leaves n a work surface so that there are no holes (one lengthwise and the other widthwise). Place ¼ cup f the untuna mixture in the center, followed by a tmat slice. Sprinkle with coarse sea salt, fresh cracked pepper and the chives (if using). Fold in the bttm, fllwed by the sides and secure with a toothpick r bamboo skewer and serve.

Roasted Carrt-Jalapen Salsa with Pepitas

Ingredients

- 1 pound carrts unpeeled and cut int 1/2-inch-thick matchsticks
- 1 medium jalapeno halved
- 1 tablespoon olive oil
- 1/2 teaspoon sea salt
- 1/4 teaspn ground cumin
- 1/4 teaspoon chili powder
- 1/4 teaspoon dried oregano
- 2 tablespoons pepitas
- 2 tablespns fresh lime juice

Directins:

1. Preheat the oven t 425 degrees F.

2. n a parchment-lined baking sheet, toss the carrots, jalapenos, olive oil, sea salt, cumin, chili powder, and oregano together until well combines. Arrange in an even layer on the baking sheet, making sure the jalapen is cut-side down. Roast in the ven until the carrots are tender and caramelized, 30 minutes.

3. Remove the pan frm the oven and reserve the jalapenos n a cutting board. Transfer the carrots to a high powered blender r food processor. When the peppers are cl enough to touch, remove the seeds and ribs with a spoon or pairing knife and discard. Add the flesh to the carrts, alng with the pepitas, lime juice, and 1/2 cup f water. Puree until smooth, adding mre water as needed to reach the consistency f tomato sauce. Taste for seasning and add more salt as necessary.

a.   Serve the salsa alngside tortilla chips
and crudités.

Crazy Gd Coconut il "Chocolate" Bark

Ingredients

- 1/2 cup cocoa r caca pwder, sifted if necessary

- 1/4 cup pure maple syrup

- 1 tablespoon smooth almond butter, optional

- pinch fine sea salt

- 1/4 cup raw hazelnuts

- 1/4 cup raw almonds

- 1/3 cup large flake dried ccnut

- 1/2 cup virgin coconut oil

Directions

1. Preheat oven to 300F. Line a 9" square pan or a small baking sheet with tw pieces of

parchment paper, ne going each way. Set aside.

2. Add hazelnuts and almonds n a baking sheet and rast in the oven for 10 minutes. Remove baking sheet and add the ccnut flakes and spread ut. Cntinue roasting the nuts and coconut flakes for anther 3-4 minutes, r until the ccnut is lightly golden. Watch closely to avid burning - coconut burns fast!

3. Place hazelnuts n several sheets of damp paper towel. Wrap the hazelnuts and rub them vigorously with the paper towel until the skins fall off. It's k if sme skins don't come ff. Discard the skins and roughly chp the hazelnuts and almnds.

4. In a medium saucepan, melt the ccnut il over lw heat. Remove frm heat and whisk in the cocoa (or cacao) powder, maple syrup, and almnd butter (if using) until smooth. Add a

pinch of sea salt to taste. Stir in half of the
almnds and hazelnuts.

5. With a spatula, spoon the chocolate mixture
    nt the prepared parchment-lined pan or sheet
    and smooth out until it's about 1/4-1/2 inch
    thick. Sprinkle on the remaining nuts and all of
    the ccnut flakes. Place into freezer on a flat
    surface for about 15 minutes, until frozen
    solid.

Baba Ganush

Ingredients

- 3 medium-sized eggplants
- 1/2 cup (130g) tahini (sesame paste)
- 1 1/4 teaspoons coarse salt
- 3 tablespoons freshly-squeezed lemon juice
- 3 cloves garlic, peeled and smashed
- 1/8 teaspn chile powder
- 1 tablespoon live oil
- a half bunch picked flat-leaf parsley or cilantro leaves

Direction

1. Preheat the oven to 375F (190C).
2. Prick each eggplant a few times, then char the outside f the eggplants by placing them directly n the flame of a gas burner and as the skin chars, turn them until the eggplants are

uniformly-charred on the outside. (If you don't have a gas stove, yu can char them under the briler. If not, skip to the next step.)

3. Place the eggplants n a baking sheet and roast in the oven for 20 t 30 minutes, until they're completely soft; you shuld be able t easily pke a paring knife int them and meet no resistance.

Dijn Baked Chicken Fingers

Ingredients

- 1/4 cup Dijon mustard

- 2 garlic cloves minced

- 2 eggs

- 1 pound boneless skinless chicken breast cut int strips

- 3 cups gluten-free cornflakes preferably rganic, non-GM

- 1/2 teaspoon paprika

- 1/2 teaspn sea salt

- 1 tablespoon olive oil

Directins:

1. Preheat the ven t 425 degrees F. Line a baking sheet with parchment paper.

2. In a small food processor, pulse the cornflakes
    with the salt and paprika until finely ground.
    Remve to a shallow bwl and drizzle in the
    olive oil. Whisk with a frk until the crnflake
    crumbs are coated and nt clumping together.
3. In a second bwl, beat the eggs until smooth.
4. In a large mixing bwl, combine the Dijon and
    garlic. Add the chicken and toss until well
    coated.
5. Working ne by one, dredge the chicken in the
    cornflake mixture, shaking ff any excess. Dip
    the tenders in the egg and return them to the
    cornflakes, pressing down until fully coated.
    Arrange the tenders in an even layer n the
    baking sheet.
6. Bake in the oven until glden and crispy, 15 to
    20 minutes. Allow to cl slightly on the tray,
    then serve alongside ketchup and mustard.

Egg & New Potato Salad

Ingredients

- Handful chopped parsley

- Hard boiled egg

- Bag of wild rocket

- Cucumber, diced, to serve

- Hot boiled new ptates

- 2 tbsp olive oil

- Juice of ½ lemon

Methd

1. Tss some hot boiled new potatoes with the live il, lemon juice and parsley. Leave to cl, then toss with quartered hard-

2. boiled eggs. Toss with wild rocket leaves and some diced cucumber to serve.

Healthy fish & chips with tartare sauce

Ingredients

- Small handful of parsley
- Leaves, chopped
- 1 tbsp capers, chopped
- 2 heaped tbsp 0% greek yogurt
- Lemon
- Wedge, t serve
- 450g potatoes, peeled and cut into chips
- 1 tbsp olive oil, plus a little extra fr brushing
- 2 white fish fillets abut 140g/5oz each
- Grated zest and juice 1 lemon

Method

1. Heat oven to 200C/fan 180C/gas 6.Toss chips in oil.Spread over a baking sheet in an even layer, bake fr 40 mins until brwned and crisp. Put the fish in a shallow dish, brush lightly

with oil, salt and pepper. Sprinkle with half the lemn juice, bake fr 12-15 mins. After 10 mins sprinkle over a little parsley and lemon zest to finish cooking.

2. Meanwhile, mix the capers, yogurt, and remaining parsley and lemn juice tgether, set aside and season if you wish. To serve, divide the chips between plates,

3. ift the fish onto the plates and serve with a spoonful of yogurt mix.

Perfect Scrambled Eggs Recipe

Ingredients

- A knb of butter

- 2 large free range eggs

- 6 tbsp single cream or full cream milk

Methd

1. Lightly whisk 2 large eggs, 6 tbsp single cream or full cream milk and a pinch of salt tgether until the mixture has just one cnsistency.

2. Heat a small non-stick frying pan fr a minute r so, then add a knob of butter and let it melt. Dn't allow the butter to brwn or it will disclur the eggs.

3. Pour in the egg mixture and let it sit, without stirring, for 20 seconds. Stir with a wooden spn, lifting and folding it over from the bottom f the pan.

4. Let it sit for anther 10 seconds then stir and
    fld again.

5. Repeat until the eggs are softly set and
    slightly runny in places. Remove from the heat
    and leave fr a moment t finish cking.

6. Give a final stir and serve the velvety scramble
    without delay.

Peanut Butter and Jelly Smthie

Ingredients:

- 1 cup frzen mixed berries

- 1 tablespn chia seeds (ptinal)

- 1 tablespn hney r maple syrup (ptinal)

- Ice cubes (ptinal)

- 2 ripe bananas

- 2 tablespns peanut butter

- 1 cup unsweetened almnd milk (r milk f yur chice)

Directins:

1. In a blender, cmbine the ripe bananas, peanut butter, almnd milk, frzen mixed berries, chia seeds (if using), and hney r maple syrup (if using).

2. Blend n high speed until smth and creamy. If desired, add a few ice cubes and blend again until chilled.

3. Taste and adjust the sweetness by adding mre hney r maple syrup if desired.

4. Pur int glasses and serve immediately, garnished with a dllp f peanut butter and a drizzle f jelly.

5. Nte: Yu can custmize this smthie by using different nut butters r types f berries fr variatin.

Greek Ygurt Parfait with Lw-FDMAP Granla and Berries

Ingredients:

- 1 cup fresh berries (e.g., strawberries, blueberries, raspberries)

- 2 tablespns hney r maple syrup (ptinal)

- 1 cup Greek ygurt (plain r flavred)

- 1/2 cup lw-FDMAP granla (check label fr FDMAP ingredients)

Directins:

1. In tw glasses r bwls, layer half f the Greek ygurt at the bttm.

2. Add half f the lw-FDMAP granla n tp f the ygurt.

3. Add half f the fresh berries n tp f the granla.

4. Repeat the layers with the remaining ingredients.

5. Drizzle hney r maple syrup n tp, if desired, fr added sweetness.

6. Serve chilled.

7. Nte: Yu can custmize this parfait by adding additinal tppings such as nuts, seeds, r ccnut flakes.

Lw FDMAP Lunch Recipes

Ingredients:

- 1/4 cup diced red bell pepper

- 1 tablespn live il

- 1 tablespn balsamic vinegar

- Salt and pepper

- 2 cups chpped lettuce

- 1 cup diced cked chicken

- 1/2 avcad, diced

Directins:

1. In a cking bwl, cmbine the chpped lettuce, diced cked chicken, diced avcad, and diced red bell pepper.

2. In a separate cking bwl, whisk tgether the live il, balsamic vinegar, salt, and pepper.

3. Pur the sauce ver the salad and tss t cmbine thrughly.

Turkey and Swiss Cheese Sandwich

Ingredients:

- 2 slices gluten-free bread

- 2 slices rasted turkey

- 2 slices Swiss cheese

- 1 tablespn maynnaise

- 1 teaspn Dijn mustard

- Lettuce and tmat fr serving

Directins:

1. Tast the gluten-free bread slices.

2. Spread the maynnaise and DIJn mustard n ne slice f the tasted bread.

3. Layer the rasted turkey, Swiss cheese, lettuce, and tmat n tp f the spread.

4. Garnish with the ther slice f tasted bread.

Irish Sda Bread (

Ingredients:

- 1/2 cup tapica starch

- 1 1/2 tablespns pwdered dextrse (r 1 Tbsp.
  sugar)

- 1 teaspn baking sda

- 1 teaspn baking pwder

- 1/2 teaspn salt

- scant 1 cup milk r nn-dairy substitute

- 1 tablespn vinegar r lemn juice

- 1 large egg, lightly beaten

- 1 tablespn grapeseed il, light live il r canla il

- 1 1/2 cups white rice flur

Directins:

1.

2. Preheat ven t 350 degrees F. Grease and flur a 9" cake pan r a 9" x 5" laf pan.

3. Place the 1 T vinegar r lemn juice int a glass measuring cup. Pur enugh milk int the measuring cup t equal 1 cup ttal. Stir the tw ingredients and let sit fr 2 minutes.

4. Cmbine the milk mix, the egg and the il int a medium sized bwl.

5. In a larger bwl, place the rice flur, tapica starch, sugar r dextrse, baking pwder, baking sda and salt. Mix these tgether and then add the milk mixture and stir well with a wden spn.

6. Pur int the baking pan and bake fr 20-25 minutes until glden brwn. Insert a knife int the center t check fr dneness.

7. Cl in the pan fr 15 minutes then turn nt a plate and serve warm.

Pumpkin Pancakes

Ingredients:

- 2 teaspns baking sda

- ½ teaspn nutmeg, grund

- 3 teaspns baking pwder

- ½ teaspn ginger, grund

- ¼ teaspn salt

- 4 tablespns brwn sugar

- ¾ cup fresh pumpkin puree

- 3 tablespns neutral il

- 5 tablespns water

- 3 cups almnd milk

- 2 cups all-purpse flur, gluten-free

- 1 large egg

- 2 ½ teaspns cinnamn, grund

Directins:

1. Mix all f the dry ingredients tgether in a large bwl.

2. Place the wet ingredients in a separate bwl and stir well. Cmbine the tw mixtures tgether until a smth cnsistency is btained.

3. Heat a tablespn f neutral il such as canla r sunflwer il in a large frying pan ver medium heat. Pur ¼ cup f the batter int the pan and ck fr abut 2 minutes r until glden brwn.

4. Flip the pancakes and ck fr anther 2 minutes.

5. Repeat these steps t ck the remaining batter. Serve with a drizzle f pure maple syrup and desired tppings.

Berry Quina Prridge

Ingredients:

- 250 milliliters water

- 5 teaspns pure maple syrup

- 188 milliliters almnd milk

- 85 grams quina

- 20 pieces fresh blueberries

- 2 teaspns canla il

- ¼ teaspn cinnamn, grund

- 10 pieces fresh raspberries

Directins:

1. Place quina in a fine mesh sieve and wash it fr 2 minutes under running water.

2. Put washed quina in a saucepan and add canla il. ver medium heat, tast quina lightly fr abut 2 minutes.

3. Add water t the tasted quina and bring it t a bil. Reduce heat t lw and put a lid n the saucepan.

4. Ck quina fr 15 minutes r until it becmes fluffy. Remve excess water, if there are any.

5. Add milk, maple syrup and cinnamn int the saucepan and bring the prridge int a simmer. Allw t ck fr anther 5 minutes.

6. Transfer the prridge int bwls and serve with berries n tp.

Breakfast Muesli

Ingredients:

- 7 tablespns live il

- 8 tablespns dried ccnut, shredded

- 65 grams brwn sugar

- 5 tablespns pumpkin seeds

- 250 grams lw FDMAP crnflakes, gluten-free

- 30 grams banana chips, dried

- 38 grams quina puffs

Directins:

1. Set the ven t 150 degrees Celsius.

2. Crush the crnflakes rughly and place them in a large bwl tgether with pumpkin seeds, quina puffs, brwn sugar and ccnut. Cver the mixture with il.

3. Spread the mixture evenly n a rasting tray that is lined with baking paper.

4. Tast the muesli in the ven fr abut 20 minutes.
    Remember t shake the tray halfway thrugh
    the ck.

5. nce the muesli is light brwn in clr, remve the
    tray frm the ven and set aside t cl.

6. Crush the banana chips lightly and add it t the
    mixture.

Cranberry Orange Smoothie

INGREDIENTS:

- 1 tbsp. lemon juice
- 1 Tsp. pure maple syrup
- 1 cup of ice cubes
- 1⅛ cups orange juice, freshly squeezed
- 1 cup cranberries, raw
- ¼ cup almond milk, unsweetened
- 1 medium banana

DIRECTIONS:

1. Use a glass dish to squeeze orange juice and remove the seeds.
2. Transfer to a food blender and pulse cranberries, almond milk, banana, lemon juice, maple syrup, and ice until it reaches your desired consistency.
3. Divide between two glasses and enjoy immediately!

French toast

INGREDIENTS:

- 4 slices gluten-free bread of your choice

- 4 Tsp. extra virgin olive oil, separated

- 2 tbsp. pure maple syrup

- 1 cup almond milk, unsweetened

- 1⅓ cup tofu, firm and plain

- 2 Tsp. pure vanilla extract, sugar-free

DIRECTIONS:

1. Use a food blender to pulse vanilla extract, almond milk, and tofu until a smooth consistency.

2. Add 2 teaspoons of olive oil into a large skillet and warm.

3. Transfer the wet mix to a shallow dish and immerse the bread in it for 60 seconds on each side. Transfer to a plate until ready to brown.

4. Cook 2 slices at once for 3 minutes on each
    side, then transfer to a serving platter.

5. Repeat for remaining slices of bread until
    complete.

6. Top with maple syrup and enjoy while warm.

Green Hibiscus Smoothie

INGREDIENTS:

- 1 cup zucchini, cubed

- ½ cup raspberries, Frozen

- ½ cup of coconut milk, liquid

- 1 hibiscus tea bag

- ½ inch ginger root, peeled

- ½ cup of water

DIRECTIONS:

1. Empty water into a mug and nuke in the microwave for 1 minute.

2. Insert the tea bag and allow it to steep for 5 minutes.

3. In the meantime, scrub zucchini and chop into small cubes. Transfer to a food blender.

4. Wash raspberries and shake to remove excess water. Transfer to the food blender. Remove

5. Remove tea bag from the water, and empty it

    into the blender.

6. Combine ginger and coconut milk in the

    blender and pulse for approximately 30

    seconds or until smooth.

7. Transfer to two glasses and enjoy

    immediately!

Hearty Oatmeal

INGREDIENTS:

- ½ Tsp. ground cloves

- 1 Tsp. ground cinnamon

- 4 tbsp. chia seeds

- ½ Tsp. ground nutmeg

- 4 tbsp. pure maple syrup

- 4 cups of water

- ½ Tsp. iodized salt

- 2 cups gluten-free rolled oats

DIRECTIONS:

1. Empty salt and water into a saucepan and warm on the highest heat setting until it starts to bubble.

2. Combine oats into hot water and heat for 5 minutes while occasionally tossing.

3. Blend ground cloves, chia seeds, ground
    cinnamon, ground nutmeg, and maple syrup,
    then warm for another 5 minutes.

4. Serve immediately and enjoy!

Immune Boosting Smoothie

INGREDIENTS:

- ⅛ Tsp. iodized salt

- 2 medium cucumber

- 2 tbsp. lime juice

- 2 cups ice

- 2 cups spinach

- 1-inch ginger root, peeled

- 2 kale leaves

- 2 medium rib celery

DIRECTIONS:

1. Thoroughly rinse spinach, celery, and kale, then shake to remove any extra water. Remove the tough ends of the kale and discard.

2. Scrub cucumbers well and chop into small sections.

3. Use a food blender to pulse salt, lime juice, ginger, cucumbers, celery, kale, and spinach until a smooth consistency.

4. Combine ice and continue to pulse until it reaches your desired consistency.

5. Distribute to two glasses and enjoy it immediately!

Peanut Butter and Banana Overnight Oats

INGREDIENTS:

- 4 tbsp. peanut butter, natural and no sugar added
- 2 cups almond milk, unsweetened
- 1 Tsp. ground cinnamon
- 2 cups gluten-free rolled oats
- 4 Tsp. chia seeds
- 2 medium bananas, mashed

DIRECTIONS:

1. Blend cinnamon, almond milk, peanut butter, bananas, chia seeds, and oats in a glass dish.
2. Toss to combine fully and cover with a layer of plastic wrap.
3. Transfer to the refrigerator and serve the next morning immediately if you desire it cold. If you prefer hot, nuke in the microwave for 60 seconds before enjoying.

Scrambled Tofu

INGREDIENTS:

- 1 Tsp. ground turmeric

- 2 cup carrots, chopped finely

- 1 tbsp. garlic-infused olive oil

- 1 Lb. pre-pressed tofu, firm

- 1 cup of water

- 4 Tsp. gluten-free soy sauce*

DIRECTIONS:

1. Use a glass dish to blend turmeric, soy sauce, and water until integrated.

2. Scrub carrots and chop into small sections. Transfer to the dish.

3. Break apart tofu into smaller sections into the dish, then toss to combine fully.

4. Empty garlic-infused olive oil into a skillet and warm over the medium setting of heat.

5. Distribute the mixture into the pan and occasionally toss while it heats for 5 minutes.

6. Remove w/ a slotted spoon and serve
   immediately. Enjoy!

Sweet Potato Toast

INGREDIENTS:

- 2 large sweet potatoes

- 2 tbsp. pure maple syrup

DIRECTIONS:

1. Set your oven to 400°F. Layer a flat sheet with baking paper.

2. Section sweet potatoes in halves lengthwise, then slice each half into thin pieces.

3. Transfer to the prepped sheet and heat for 20 minutes.

4. Drizzle with maple syrup and enjoy!

Breakfast Burritos

Ingredients

- 3 eggs

- ½ cup about 100ml coconut milk (check labels)

- 2tbsp coconut flur, sifted

- 1tsp coconut oil

- ½ tsp arrwrt pinch f salt

- Coconut il or live oil fr pan

Filling

- 2tbsp olive oil

- 350g rump steak, finely chopped

- ½ red chilli, seeds remved, finely chopped

- 1 tomato, diced

- dash Tabasco sauce pinch cayenne pepper

- small handful fresh coriander, chopped

Directins:

1. Make the trtillas. Whisk the tortilla ingredients together in a bwl. Let the mixture sit fr 10 minutes while the pan heats so the ccnut flour can absorb the liquid, then whisk again.
2. Heat a crepe pan or frying pan ver a medium-high heat.
3. Melt a small amount f oil in the pan, swirling to coat the bottom and sides.
4. Pour ¼ of the batter int the hot pan, turning the pan in a circular motion with ne hand so t spread the batter thinly arund the pan.
5. Ck fr 1 minute until the edges start t lift and turn golden. Gently wrk a spatula under the crepe and flip it over. Cook on the second side for 15 seconds and turn out on a plate.
6. Repeat with the remaining batter
7. To make the filling sauté the steak, chilli and tomato and fry until the meat is golden and

cooked thrugh, abut 4 minutes. Add the remaining ingredients and seasn to taste.

8. T assemble the burrito, place the warmed tortillas n serving plates and divide the steak between them. You could top with a little lettuce too. Rll up to serve

Sundried Tomato and live Muffins

Ingredients

- 8 olives, pitted and chopped

- 4 fresh basil leaves, finely chpped

- 75g dairy-free spread or coconut il, melted

- 2 large eggs, beaten

- 1 tbsp sun dried tomato paste

- 150ml dairy-free milk r lactose free milk (check labels)

- 225g self raising gluten free flour

- 1 tsp gluten-free baking powder

- ¼ tsp xanthan gum

- ½ tsp salt

- 80g hard cheese or lw lactose cheese, grated

- 40g or 5 drained, bttled sun-dried tomatoes, finely chopped

Instruction

1. Preheat the ven t 180°C, gas 4. Line a muffin
    tin with paper cases

2. Place the flur, baking pwder, xanthan gum
    and salt into a mixing bwl and stir thoroughly.
    Add the dairy-free cheese, sun-dried tmates,
    olives and basil leaves and mix well.

3. Mix together the melted spread or oil, eggs,
    tomato purée and dairy-free milk.

4. Pur the egg mixture int the flur mixture and
    gently mix in. Spoon the mixture into the
    muffin cases.

5. Bake fr about 25-30 minutes until glden
    brown. Remove from the oven and place on a
    cl rack. Delicious eaten hot or cold

Paleo Fcaccia Bread

Ingredients

- 1tsp baking pwder

- Handful f chpped fresh herbs - thyme, or rosemary work well. live il, for brushing

- Additinal coarse sea salt, fr topping

- Chopped lives and cherry tomatoes for tpping

- 4 large eggs

- ¼ cup coconut cream - taken frm the top f a can f ccnut milk

- ¼ cup coconut flour

- ½ teaspn bicarbonate f soda

Instruction

1. Preheat oven to 180C, gas mark 4.

2. Beat the eggs with the coconut cream until smth. In a medium bowl, cmbine the ccnut flour, salt, baking powder and sda. Add the

egg mixture t the flour and stir until well combined. Make sure there are no lumps

3. Stir in a handful of fresh herbs e.g rosemary

4. Line a round cake tin r small square traybake tin with parchment and spread the batter in the pan. Drizzle with live oil. Top with herbs, lives and cherry tmates.

5. Bake for 15-20 minutes until top is lightly browned. Remve frm the oven and brush with more olive oil. Cool before slicing and serving.

Thai-Style Rice And Meat Noodles

INGREDIENTS

- 200g sirloin steak
- 60g rice ndles
- 115g broccoli
- ½ carrot, grated
- 45g soybeans
- 1 tbsp mint, finely chopped
- salt
- tablespoons of lime juice
- 1 tbsp fish sauce
- 1 tbsp olive oil
- 1 tbsp sugar
- 1/2 chili

DIRECTINS:

1. Marinate the meat

2. Pour the lime juice, fish sauce, il, sugar, and chili int a bwl.

3. Mix everything well.

4. Take 2 tablespns of this marinade and put them in a bwl and set the rest aside.

5. Arrange the meat and turn it over to sprinkle it well with the marinade.

6. Cover and leave to rest in the refrigerator for an hour.

7. Cook the spaghetti and brccli

8. Cook the spaghetti al dente in a pot of boiling salted water. Drain them and pur them into a bwl.

9. Ck the brccli al dente in a pt f boiling salted water. Drain them and put them in the salad bwl.

10. Add the carrot, bean spruts, and mint, season with the reserved marinade, and mix.

11. Cook the meat on the barbecue or in a pan
and cut it into thin slices. Then arrange them
in the salad bwl.

Cherry Mug Cake

INGREDIENTS

- ¼ cup golden flaxseed meal

- ½ tsp baking powder

- 2 eggs whites nly

- 10 frozen tart cherries (or fresh, pitted)

- 1 medium banana

- ¾ cup raw, shell-free sunflower seeds (or
almond meal)

DIRECTINS:

1. In a bowl r immersin blender cup, blend
tgether the cherries, egg whites, and banana.

You can also do this in a blender. Blend until a smoothie-like consistency.

2. In yur large microwave-safe bowl, combine the flax seed meal, ground sunflower seeds (r almond meal), and baking powder.

3. Pour in the cherry mixture, and mix until the wet and dry ingredients are fully combined.

4. Place the mug in the microwave and microwave on high fr 3 to 3.5 minutes.

5. Serve immediately, and enjy! This mug cake goes great with a scoop of sugar-free ice cream.

Spinach and Feta melets

Ingredients:

- 2 tablespns chpped fresh herbs (such as parsley r dill)

- Salt and pepper t taste

- 1 tablespn live il

- 4 large eggs

- 1 cup fresh spinach leaves, rughly chpped

- 1/4 cup crumbled feta cheese

Directins:

1. In a medium-sized mixing bwl, crack the eggs and whisk them until well beaten. Seasn with salt and pepper accrding t yur taste.

2. Heat the live il in a nn-stick skillet ver medium heat.

3. Add the chpped spinach t the skillet and sauté fr 1-2

4. minutes, until wilted.

5. Pur the beaten eggs ver the spinach, tilting the skillet t spread the eggs evenly. Allw the eggs t ck undisturbed fr a minute r tw, until the edges start t set.

6. Sprinkle the crumbled feta cheese evenly ver the eggs, fllwed by the chpped fresh herbs.

7. Using a spatula, carefully fld ne side f the melet ver the filling. Cntinue t ck fr anther minute r until the eggs are fully set and the cheese has melted.

8. Slide the melet nt a serving plate and repeat the prcess t make the secnd melet.

9. Serve the Spinach and Feta melets ht, garnished with additinal fresh herbs if desired.

Turkey sausage Breakfast Sandwich

Ingredients:

- 1 tablespn maynnaise

- 1 teaspn Dijn mustard

- Salt and pepper t taste

- Cking spray r butter fr cking

- 2 slices f gluten-free bread (r bread f yur chice)

- 2 turkey sausage patties

- 1 large egg

- 1 slice f cheddar cheese

Directins:

1. Preheat a nn-stick skillet ver medium heat and lightly cat it with cking spray r butter.

2. Ck the turkey sausage patties accrding t the package Directins: until they are glden brwn and cked thrugh.

3. Meanwhile, in a small bwl, whisk the egg with salt and pepper t taste.

4. Pur the beaten egg int the skillet and ck, gently stirring ccasinally, until it is fully cked and scrambled. Remve frm heat.

5. Tast the bread slices until they are glden brwn.

6. In a separate small bwl, mix the maynnaise and Dijn mustard until well cmbined.

7. Spread the maynnaise-mustard mixture n ne side f each tasted bread slice.

8. n ne slice f bread, place the cked turkey sausagc patties.

9. Tp the sausage patties with the scrambled egg.

10. Place the cheddar cheese slice n tp f the scrambled egg.

11. Finally, cver the sandwich with the remaining slice f bread, may-mustard side dwn.

12. Gently press the sandwich tgether.

13. Serve the Turkey Sausage Breakfast Sandwich

immediately and enjy!

Buckwheat breakfast bwl with chia seeds, nuts, and almnd milk:

Ingredients:

- 1/4 cup mixed nuts (such as almnds, pecans, r walnuts)

- 1/2 cup almnd milk

- 1 tablespn hney (ptinal)

- 1 cup cked buckwheat

- 1 tablespn chia seeds

Directins:

1. In a bwl, cmbine the cked buckwheat, chia seeds, and mixed nuts.
2. Add almnd milk and stir until well cmbined.
3. Drizzle hney ver the tp if desired.
4. Serve cld r warmed up.

Gluten-free banana bread with scrambled eggs and turkey sausage:

Ingredients:

- 1/4 cup ccnut il r butter, melted

- 1/4 cup maple syrup

- 1 teaspn vanilla extract

- 4-6 turkey sausage links, cked

- Scrambled eggs

- 1 cup gluten-free flur

- 1 teaspn baking pwder

- 1/4 teaspn salt

- 2 ripe bananas, mashed

- 2 eggs

Directins:

1. Preheat the ven t 350°F.

2. In a mixing bwl, whisk tgether the gluten-free flur, baking pwder, and salt.

3. Add the mashed bananas, eggs, melted ccnut
    il r butter, maple syrup, and vanilla extract,
    and mix until well cmbined.

4. Pur the batter int a greased laf pan and bake
    fr 40-45 minutes, until a tthpick inserted int
    the center cmes ut clean.

5. Let the banana bread cl fr 10 minutes befre
    slicing.

6. Serve the banana bread slices with cked
    turkey sausage links and scrambled eggs.

Breakfast parfait with Greek ygurt, gluten-free granla, and mixed berries:

Ingredients*:*
- 1/2 cup mixed berries (such as strawberries, blueberries, r raspberries)

- 1 cup Greek ygurt

- 1/2 cup gluten-free granla

Directins:

1. Spn the Greek ygurt int a bwl r jar.

2. Tp with gluten-free granla and mixed berries.

3. Serve chilled.

Gluten-free bagel with smked salmn, cream cheese, and capers:

Ingredients:

- 2 tablespns cream cheese

- 1 tablespn capers

- 1 **gluten**-free bagel

- 2 unces smked salmn

Directins:

1. Tast the gluten-free bagel.

2. Spread cream cheese n bth halves f the bagel.

3. Tp with smked salmn and capers.

4. Serve pen-faced.

Simple Grain-Free Granola

Ingredients

- 1 1/2 tsp ground cinnamn (ptinal)

- 2 Tbsp coconut, cane, r muscavado sugar

- 1/4 tsp sea salt

- 3 Tbsp coconut or olive il

- 1/3 scant cup maple syrup (or sub agave or honey if not vegan)

- 1/4 cup dried blueberries (ptinal // or other dried fruit)

- 1/4 cup roasted unsalted sunflower seeds (ptinal)

- 1/2 cup unsweetened coconut flake

- 2 cups slivered raw almonds (slivered almnds d best here)

- 1 1/4 cup raw pecans

- 1 cup raw walnuts

- 3 Tbsp chia seeds

- 1 Tbsp flaxseed meal

Directins:

1. Preheat oven to 325 degrees F (162 C) and position a rack in the center f the oven.

2. In a large mixing bowl, combine the coconut, nuts, chia seeds, flax seed, cinnamn, ccnut sugar, and salt.

3. In a small saucepan ver lw heat, warm the ccnut oil and maple syrup and pour ver the dry ingredients and mix well.

4. Spread the mixture evenly onto a large baking sheet (may require two depending on size) and bake for 20 minutes. Then remve from ven, add dried blueberries and roasted sunflower seeds, and stir.

5. Increase heat to 340 degrees F (171 C) and return t oven for another 5-8 minutes, r until deep glden brwn.

6. The coconut oil will help this granla crisp up nicely, but be sure to watch it carefully as it brwns quickly.

7. nce the granla is visibly browned and dne cking (about 27 minutes total for me), remove from the oven and let cool cmpletely.

8. Stre in a cntainer with an air-tight seal, and it shuld keep for a few weeks.

Quinoa Berry Breakfast Bake

Ingredients

- 1 tsp butter/oil for greasing pan

- 1.5 cup quina dry/uncked

- 1.5 cups strawberries

- 1 cup blueberries

- 1/2 cup raspberries

- 1/4 cup walnuts chopped (or more)

- 3 eggs

- 3 cups lactose-free milk

- 1/4 cup maple syrup r brown sugar

- 1 tbsp cinnamon

- 1 tsp ginger

- Low fodmap quinoa berry breakfast bake

Directins:

1. Preheat yur oven to 375 degrees F.

2. Grease a large baking dish with butter or il.
   Pour the quinoa into the dish and lightly shake
   t distribute the quinoa evenly.

3. Slice the strawberries. Sprinkle the berries
   and walnuts over the quina in the dish.

4. In a large bowl whisk the eggs. Stir the milk,
   syrup and spices into the eggs. Gently pur
   over the quinoa mixture.

5. Bake in preheated oven for 1 hur until the
   quinoa has absorbed all f the liquid. Extra
   servings can be kept in the fridge fr up t 5
   days or the freezer for mnths.

Super Simple Roasted Carrot Sup!

Ingredients

- 1 sprig of thyme or 1/4 tsp. dried

- 1/2 tsp dSSried chives (substitute 1/2 nin chopped)

- 1 stem rganic celery, chpped into 2-inch pieces

- Salt and freshly grund pepper to taste

- 1/4 tsp grund cinnamon

- 6-8 large carrots

- 3 tablespoons extra virgin olive il

- 3 cups organic chicken bone broth (substitute vegetable broth fr vegan)

- 1 piece ginger (1/2 inch long piece, peeled

Directins:

1. Preheat oven t 375 degrees F.

2. Peel and slice carrots into 3-inch pieces. Set
    on a baking sheet pan, sprinkle with about 2
    tablespoons live il. Seasn with salt and
    pepper. Place in oven for 45 minutes t 1 hour
    until roasted and frk tender. Then set aside t
    cl.

3. While the carrts are roasting, place 1
    tablespoon olive oil in a pot/soup pot on
    medium-lw heat. Place the chopped celery in
    the pot and ck and stir for about 5 minutes
    until celery is translucent. Add the thyme,
    ginger, chives (r nin), and cinnamn (optional)
    and cook for anther minute. Add the organic
    chicken bone broth (recipe fr homemade n
    this site) to the celery mixture and bring t a
    simmer for 5-10 minutes. Add the cooked
    carrots.

4. Blend: either use an immersion blender right
    in the soup pt or use a quality blender.*

Blend until creamy and desired consistency. Add more stock r water as needed. Garnish with chopped chives, chpped nuts, a swirl of non-dairy milk.

5. Pur back into saucepan and heat on low until ready to serve.

Chia seed pudding with almnd milk and mixed berries:

Ingredients:

- 1/2 teaspn vanilla extract

- 1/2 cup mixed berries

- 1/4 cup chia seeds

- 1 cup almnd milk

Directins:

1. In a mixing bwl, whisk tgether the chia seeds, almnd milk, and vanilla extract.

2. Let the mixture sit fr at least 30 minutes, stirring ccasinally, until the chia seeds have absrbed the liquid and the mixture has thickened t a pudding cnsistency.

3. Serve the chia seed pudding tpped with mixed berries.

**Gluten-free breakfast sandwich with egg,
cheese, and turkey sausage:**

Ingredients:

- 1-2 turkey sausage links, cked

- Salt and pepper t taste

- 1 gluten-free English muffin

- 1 egg

- 1 slice cheese

Directins:

1. Tast the gluten-free English muffin.

2. Ck the egg in a skillet ver medium heat t yur
   desired preference (scrambled, ver-easy, etc.).

3. Place the cked egg n ne half f the tasted
   English muffin

4. Tp with a slice f cheese and cked turkey
   sausage links.

5. Seasn with salt and pepper t taste.

6. Tp with the ther half f the tasted English muffin.

7. Serve ht.

Shakshuka with gluten-free tast:

Ingredients:

- 1/4 teaspn cayenne pepper

- 1 can (14 z) diced tmates

- Salt and pepper t taste

- 4-6 eggs

- Gluten-free tast

- 1 tablespn live il

- 1/2 nin, chpped

- 1 bell pepper, chpped

- 2 garlic clves, minced

- 1 teaspn paprika

- 1/2 teaspn cumin

Directins:

1. Heat the live il in a large skillet ver medium
   heat.

2. Add the chpped nin and bell pepper, and sauté until sft, about 5-7 minutes.

3. Add the minced garlic, paprika, cumin, and cayenne pepper, and stir until fragrant, abut 1 minute.

4. Pur in the diced tmates and seasn with salt and pepper t taste.

5. Bring the mixture t a simmer and let it ck fr 10-15 minutes, until the sauce has thickened.

6. Make small wells in the tmat sauce with a spn and crack an egg int each well.

7. Cver the skillet with a lid and let the eggs ck fr 5-7 minutes, until the whites are set but the ylks are still runny.

8. Serve ht with gluten-free tast.

Breakfast smthie with almnd milk, mixed berries, and prtein pwder:

Ingredients:

- 1 scp prtein pwder

- 1 tablespn hney (ptinal)

- 1 cup almnd milk

- 1/2 cup mixed berries (such as strawberries, blueberries, r raspberries)

Directins:

1. In a blender, cmbine the almnd milk, mixed berries, prtein pwder, and hney (if using).

2. Blend until smth and creamy.

3. Serve cld.

Scrambled Eggs with Spinach Prep Time

Ingredients:

- Salt and pepper t taste

- ptinal tppings: grated cheese, diced tmates, r chpped herbs (such as parsley r chives) 4 large eggs

- 1 cup fresh spinach leaves, washed and chpped

- 1 tablespn live il

Directins:

1. In a medium-sized bwl, crack the eggs and whisk them until well beaten. Seasn with salt and pepper accrding t yur taste.

2. Heat the live il in a nn-stick skillet r frying pan ver medium heat.

3. Add the chpped spinach t the pan and sauté fr abut 1-2 minutes until it wilts slightly.

4. Pur the beaten eggs int the pan with the spinach.

5. Using a spatula, gently stir and scramble the eggs with the spinach mixture. Cntinue stirring ccasinally until the eggs are cked t yur desired level f dneness.

6. This usually takes arund 3-4 minutes.

7. nce the eggs are cked, remve the pan frm heat.

8. Serve the scrambled eggs with spinach n plates r bwls. Yu can garnish them with grated cheese, diced tmates, r chpped herbs if desired.

9. Enjy the delicius and nutritius scrambled eggs with spinach while still warm.

Carrt Cake Ccnut Prridge Prep Time

Ingredients:

- 1/2 teaspn grund nutmeg

- 1/4 teaspn grund ginger

- Pinch f salt

- 2 cups unsweetened almnd milk r any plant-based milk

- Chpped nuts, shredded ccnut, r additinal raisins fr garnish (ptinal)

- 1 cup rlled ats

- 1 medium carrt, grated

- 2 tablespns shredded ccnut

- 2 tablespns raisins

- 1 tablespn maple syrup r hney (ptinal)

- 1 teaspn grund cinnamn

Directins:

1. In a medium-sized saucepan, cmbine the rlled
   ats, grated carrt, shredded ccnut, raisins,
   maple syrup r hney (if using), grund cinnamn,
   grund nutmeg, grund ginger, and a pinch f
   salt. Mix well t cmbine all the ingredients.

2. Pur the almnd milk r plant-based milk int the
   saucepan and stir until everything is well
   cmbined.

3. Place the saucepan ver medium heat and
   bring the mixture t a gentle bil. nce it starts
   biling, reduce the heat t lw and let it simmer fr
   abut 5-7 minutes, stirring ccasinally. The ats
   shuld sften and absrb the liquid, and the
   mixture will becme thick and creamy.

4. nce the desired cnsistency is reached, remve
   the saucepan frm the heat.

5. Serve the carrt cake ccnut prridge warm in
   bwls.

6. Yu can garnish it with chpped nuts, shredded
   ccnut, r additinal raisins if desired.

7. Enjy yur delicius and nurishing carrt cake

ccnut prridge!

Bacn and Zucchini Crustless Quiche

Ingredients:

- 4 large eggs

- 1 cup milk (dairy r nn-dairy)

- 1/2 teaspn salt

- 1/4 teaspn black pepper

- 6 slices f bacn, cked and crumbled

- 1 medium zucchini, grated

- 1 cup shredded cheddar cheese

- 1/2 cup chpped scallins

Directins:

1. Preheat yur ven t 375°F (190°C). Grease a 9-inch pie dish r a similar-sized baking dish and set aside.

2. In a skillet, ck the bacn until crispy. Remve the bacn frm the pan and let it cl. nce cled, crumble the bacn int small pieces.

3. In the same skillet, using the bacn drippings, sauté the grated zucchini ver medium heat fr abut 3-4 minutes until it sftens slightly. Remve frm heat and set aside.

4. In a mixing bwl, whisk tgether the eggs, milk, salt, and black pepper until well cmbined.

5. Spread the grated zucchini evenly ver the bttm f the prepared pie dish. Sprinkle the crumbled bacn, shredded cheddar cheese, and chpped scallins ver the zucchini.

6. Pur the egg mixture ver the bacn and cheese, making sure it is evenly distributed.

7. Place the dish in the preheated ven and bake fr apprximately 30-35 minutes, r until the quiche is set and the tp is glden brwn.

8. nce cked, remve the quiche frm the ven and let it cl fr a few minutes befre slicing and serving.

9. Serve the Bacn and Zucchini Crustless Quiche warm as a delightful breakfast, brunch, r light lunch ptin. It can be enjyed n its wn r accmpanied by a side salad r fresh fruit.

Minestrne

INGREDIENTS

- 1 Leek - finely chopped
- 10 Cherry Tomatoes
- 1 cup Frozen Peas
- litres f Water (or vegetable stck)
- 1 cube Vegetable Bouillon
- a handful of Rice Vermicelli (r other small pasta shapes)
- Salt and freshly ground Black Pepper
- A few fresh Basil Leaves, finely chopped
- ptinal Tpping: Grated Parmesan
- 5 tablespoons Extra Virgin live il
- 1 White nion - finely chopped
- 1 clove Garlic - finely chopped
- 2 Ptates - peeled and cubed (r sweet ptates)
- 200g Pumpkin - peeled and cubed

- 2 Carrts - thickly sliced

- 1 Celery Stalk - thickly sliced

- 1 small Brccli head - cut int small pieces

- 1 Zucchini - cubed

DIRECTINS:

1. Heat the extra virgin live oil in a large pt on low fire, add the onion and garlic, and saute fr 3 minutes until the nin is translucent.

2. Add all the vegetables, the hard vegetables (carrots, potatoes, pumpkin) first, followed by softer ones, except the frzen peas, and mix well.

3. Add water and bouillon, and bring to a bil, then lower the heat and simmer gently for 30 minutes. Add the frzen peas 10 minutes before the end f the cooking time.

4. Add the rice vermicelli and boil for 1 minute. If yu are adding pasta, cook it in the soup until

al dente (abut 10 minutes) or as per the
packet's instruction.

5. Remove from the heat, season to taste, and
    stir in the basil leaves. Serve immediately in
    individual bwls, with parmesan cheese and
    garlic bread if desired

Potato Leek Soup

INGREDIENTS

- 8 cups bone brth or chicken stock r veggie stck

- 2 bay leaves

- 1½ teaspns finely chopped fresh thyme

- 1 teaspoon sea salt

- ¼ teaspn ground black pepper

- 1 cup plain cashew cream (t replace heavy dairy cream)

- 2 tablespoons Braggs apple cider vinegar

- ¾ cup of nutritinal yeast

- Chives, finely chopped (optional)

- Bacon, chopped in small cubes (ptinal)

- Grated asiago cheese (optional)

- Chili il (optional fr drizzling)

- 3 tablespns unsalted grass-fed butter, ghee, r ccnut il

- 4 washed leeks, white and green parts, rughly chopped

- 3 cloves garlic, peeled and smashed (n need t mince since yu'll be blending to finish)

- ¾ cup of cooking sherry

- 2 lbs Yukon or russet potatoes, (cauliflower for pale) scrubbed/washed well and rughly chopped into ½-inch pieces

PREPARATINS

1. Melt the butter over medium heat in a large dutch oven.

2. Add the leeks and garlic and to simmer, stirring regularly, until sft and wilted, abut 10 minutes. N browning is allwed, but sherry splashing to deglaze is encuraged.

3. Add the potatoes (or separately steamed and drained cauliflower), stock/broth of choice,

bay leaves, thyme, salt, and pepper to a pot and bring to a slow boil. Cver and turn the heat dwn t lw.

4. Simmer for 20 minutes, r until the ptates are very soft and break apart when smshed with a fork. If using cauliflower you can immediately blend after adding it cked into the broth mixture.

5. Fish out bay leaves, then add the nutritional yeast and fry the sup with a hand-held immersion blender until smooth. (Alternatively, use a standard blender to fry the soup in batches but that's a pain in the ass.)

6. Add the cashew cream and apple cider vinegar and bring t a simmer. Taste and adjust the seasning with salt and pepper.

7. Garnish whichever way you like!

Tart Cherry-Apple Crunch

INGREDIENTS

- 1 pound frozen pitted tart cherries

- 1 green apple, cored and diced

- ¼ cup light brown sugar, packed

- ½ teaspn almond extract

- 1½ tablespoons cornstarch r arrowroot powder

- ½ cup unsweetened cherry or apple juice

- Nnstick cooking spray

Topping:

- ¼ cup ld-fashined rlled oats

- ¼ cup brwn sugar

- ¼ cup walnuts, chopped

- 2 tablespoons whole-wheat pastry flour

- 3 tablespoons grapeseed oil

- ¼ teaspoon salt (optional)

DIRECTINS:

1. Preheat oven to 400°F.

2. In a bwl, tss together the cherries, apple, brown sugar, and almond extract.

3. In a cup, mix the crnstarch and juice and add t the fruit mixture, stirring well.

4. Pour the mixture into an 8-inch-square baking dish sprayed with nonstick cooking spray.

5. Mix together the remaining ingredients. Crumble the mixture on top of the fruit.

6. Bake for 30 minutes.

7. Raise heat to broil and brown topping lightly for 1-2 minutes.

8. Remve from oven. serve warm r cold.

Turkey Sausage Patties

INGREDIENTS:

- 1 tbsp. extra virgin olive oil

- ½ Tsp. rosemary seasoning

- ⅛ Tsp. black pepper

- ½ tbsp. pure maple syrup

- ½ Lb. ground turkey

- ¼ Tsp. iodized salt

- ½ Tsp. sage seasoning

DIRECTIONS:

1. Use a glass dish to combine ground turkey, salt, sage, rosemary, black pepper, and maple syrup until incorporated.

2. Heat olive oil in a large skillet on your stove's medium heat setting.

3. Form 4 evenly sized patties and arrange in the pan, then cook in batches if necessary, as you

want to leave some space in between to cook evenly.

4. Heat for approximately 6 minutes, then flips to the other side. Continue to brown for an additional 6 minutes or until cooked fully.

5. Transfer patties to a plate lined with kitchen paper to remove any excess grease.

6. Enjoy immediately!

Shrimp with Beans

INGREDIENTS:

- ½ Lb. green beans, washed and trimmed

- 2 Tbsp. olive oil

- Salt

- 1 Lb. shrimp, peeled and deveined

- 2 Tbsp. soy sauce

DIRECTIONS:

1. Heat oil in a pan.

2. Add beans to the pan and sauté for 5-6 minutes or until tender.

3. Remove pan from heat and set aside.

4. Add shrimp in the same pan and cook for 2-3 minutes each side.

5. Return beans to the pan along with soy sauce. Stir well and cook until shrimp is done.

6. Season with salt and serve.

Salmn and Quina Bwl

Ingredients:

- 1 cup chpped spinach

- 1/4 cup diced cucumber

- 1/4 cup diced red bell pepper

- 1 tablespn live il

- 1 tablespn lemn juice

- Salt and pepper

- 1/2 cup quina

- 1 cup water

- 1/2 cup cked salmn

Directins:

1. Rinse the quina under cld water.

2. In a visage pan, cmbine the quina and water thrughly.

3. Bring t a bil, then reduce the heat t lw and
    simmer fr 15-20 minutes until the quina is
    tender and the water has been absrbed.

4. In a cking bwl, cmbine the cked quina, cked
    salmn, chpped spinach, diced cucumber, and
    diced red bell pepper.

5. In a separate cking bwl, whisk tgether the live
    il, lemn juice, salt, and pepper.

6. Pur the dressing ver the quina bwl and tss t
    cmbine.

Lw FDMAP Minestrne Sup

Ingredients:

- 1/2 cup diced tmat

- 2 cups lw FDMAP vegetable brth

- 1/2 cup gluten-free pasta

- 1/4 cup chpped parsley

- Salt and pepper

- 1 tablespn live il

- 1/2 cup diced carrt

- 1/2 cup diced celery

- 1/2 cup diced zucchini

Directins:

1. Heat the cking il in a pt ver medium heat temperature.

2. Add the diced carrt, celery, zucchini, and tmat and ck fr 5-7 minutes until sftened.

3. Add the lw FDMAP vegetable brth and bring t
    a bil.

4. Add the gluten-free pasta and simmer fr 10-15
    minutes until the pasta is cked.

5. Stir in the sliced parsley and seasn with salt
    and pepper t be tasty.

Tuna Salad Lettuce Wraps

Ingredients:

- 1 can tuna, drained

- 1/4 cup diced celery

- 1/4 cup diced red bell pepper

- 2 tablespns maynnaise

- 1 tablespn Dijn mustard

- Lettuce leaves fr serving

Directins:

1. Mix well t cmbine.

2. Spn the tuna mixture nt lettuce leaves.

3. Rll up the lettuce leaves t make a wrap.

4. In a cking bwl, cmbine the drained tuna, diced celery,

5. diced red bell pepper, maynnaise, and Dijn mustard.